KU-508-027

Are You Like a Chimpanzee?

Are you like a chimpanzee?

Humans laugh ...

and so do chimpanzees.

Humans hold hands ...

and so do chimpanzees.

CHIMPS AND US

Contents

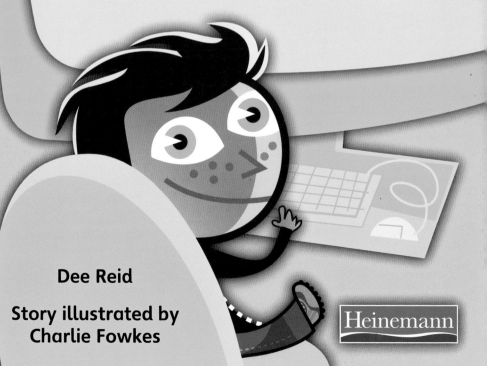

Dee Reid

Story illustrated by
Charlie Fowkes

Heinemann

Before Reading

Find out about

- How chimpanzees are like humans

Tricky words

- humans
- laugh
- hold
- each
- other
- fleas

Introduce these tricky words and help the reader when they come across them later!

Text starter

Chimpanzees do lots of things that humans do. They laugh. They hold hands. They hug each other. They even kiss! So are you like a chimpanzee?

Humans hug each other ...

and so do chimpanzees.

Humans kiss each other ...

and so do chimpanzees.

Humans hold things with their hands ...

and so do chimpanzees.

But ... chimpanzees hold things with their feet.

Do you?

Chimpanzees can pick up things with their feet too.

Chimpanzees walk on their feet ... and their hands.

Do you?

Chimpanzees pick fleas off each other and eat them.

Do you?

So are you like a chimpanzee?

Quiz

Text Detective

- Do chimpanzees kiss?
- Do humans pick fleas off each other and eat them?

Word Detective

- **Phonic Focus:** Initial letter sounds
  Page 4: Find three words that start with 'h'.
- Page 6: Find a word that rhymes with 'miss'.
- Page 8: Find a word that means 'grip'.

Super Speller

Read these words:

do   eat   so

Now try to spell them!

HA! HA! HA!

Q What kind of monkey can fly?

 A hot air baboon!

In this story

 Mr Cross

 The children

 Charlie the chimpanzee

Tricky words

- cheeky
- head
- put
- monkey
- where
- bottom

 Introduce these tricky words and help the reader when they come across them later!

Story starter

Mr Cross was a teacher. One day, he took the children to the zoo. They went to see Cheeky Charlie the chimpanzee. "Don't go near the cage," said Mr Cross. "Cheeky Charlie might try to take something."

Cheeky Charlie

Cheeky Charlie took
Mr Cross's cap.
He put the cap on his head.

Mr Cross was cross.

"You cheeky monkey!"
said Mr Cross.
"Give me back my cap."

"Ha! Ha! Ha!" said the children.

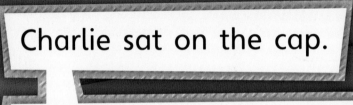

Charlie sat on the cap.

Mr Cross could not see it.

"Where is my cap?"
said Mr Cross.

"Charlie is on it,"
said the children.

Charlie put the cap on his bottom.

Charlie put the cap
on Mr Cross's head.

"Where is my cap?"
said Mr Cross.

"Ha, ha, ha!" said the children.

"Your cap is on your head!"

Quiz

Text Detective

- Where did Cheeky Charlie put Mr Cross's cap?
- Do you think 'Cheeky Charlie' is a good name for him?

Word Detective

- Phonic Focus: Initial letter sounds

  Page 13: What sound is at the beginning

  of 'Cheeky' and 'Charlie'?
- Page 14: Find a word that rhymes with 'pack'.
- Page 23: Find the word 'your' twice.

Super Speller

Read these words:

he   my   on

Now try to spell them!

HA! HA! HA!

Q How do chimpanzees make toast?

A They put bread under a gorilla.